King Midas and other...

Brian Gray

Illustrated by
Yannick Robert
Rosalind Hudson

CONTENTS

Silver Tongues 3
The Golden Fish 19
King Midas 37

OXFORD
UNIVERSITY PRESS

Dear Reader,

When I was at school I was once given a prize. The prize was a book called *Legends From The Outback*. I was so proud that I read it from cover to cover. The book was full of wonderful myths and legends told by the Aboriginal people in Australia. The stories describe Dreamtime, a time when the gods, the people and their ancestors shared the land.

Ever since reading that book, I have enjoyed exploring myths and legends from all over the world. I also write my own stories to escape into – my own dreamtime.

Here are three tales that have been retold many times by many authors. Like most myths and legends, they tell more than just a story. They also try to make sense of the world and show what is important in life.

I hope you enjoy them!

Brian Gray

Silver Tongues

A folk tale from Bolivia, in South America

Chapter 1

Long ago there was a deep valley which snaked between two mountains. The people who lived in the valley looked up at the two mountains and were thankful. The mountains brought them shelter. The mountains brought them rain. And when the snow melted on their peaks, the rivers ran from them like silver ribbons deep into the valley.

The people called the mountains Parichata and Tati-Tugui after the spirits that lived within them.

Parichata was a special mountain. It had a hidden secret. The mountain was rich in silver!

After the rains, nuggets of silver would wash down into the valley. The people would collect the silver from the river beds and make jewellery and trinkets. Then they would offer them to the mountain spirits as gifts.

• *Parichata*: (say) 'par-ee-chatter'.   • *Tati-Tugui*: (say) 'ta-tee-too-ghee'.

Chapter 2

One day, strange men from distant lands invaded the valley. They wore shining armour. They carried weapons of thunder. With their greedy eyes they scoured the lands, taking everything that they could.

They stole from the temples and put the holy men to death. They stole the crops and food to feed their armies. They stole the very peace and joy that the people of the valley had enjoyed for a thousand years.

The people were afraid of these strangers. They gave away everything they had, hoping that the invaders would go away and leave them in peace. They knew they were not strong enough to fight such powerful soldiers.

But then the strangers discovered the secret of Parichata. They forced the people to tell them where the silver came from. Then they put every man, woman and child from the valley in chains, and set them to work. They were forced deep down inside the mountain, to mine the silver. The people of the valley became slaves. They worked for many passing suns to feed the greed of their new masters.

Day after day the people cried and beat themselves in despair as their beautiful mountain was cut, gouged and torn apart. They knew that this terrible destruction would only stop when there was no more silver to mine.

They prayed to Parichata. They prayed to Tati-Tugui. But their prayers seemed to be unanswered.

Chapter 3

Then a stranger came to the valley. His skin was as dark and as rugged as the mountains themselves. His eyes were as black as the darkest storm and his hair hung in a silver-grey plait down to his waist.

He looked like a holy man, but none of the people had ever seen him before. Some said he was like one of the ancient ones, who dwelled long ago in the mountains. Stories about such people had been told by the elders for a thousand years.

The stranger worked among them, talking to them in their own language. He told them that when they prayed that night they should each put a small piece of silver in their mouth. Then, and only then, would the mountains hear their prayers.

So, on that moonlit night, as the people of the valley stumbled down the mountain in their chains, each one placed a small piece of silver on his or her tongue. They began to whisper their prayers.

As they prayed, a terrible storm began to rage. Wind and rain lashed the mountain, washing away the dust and mud.

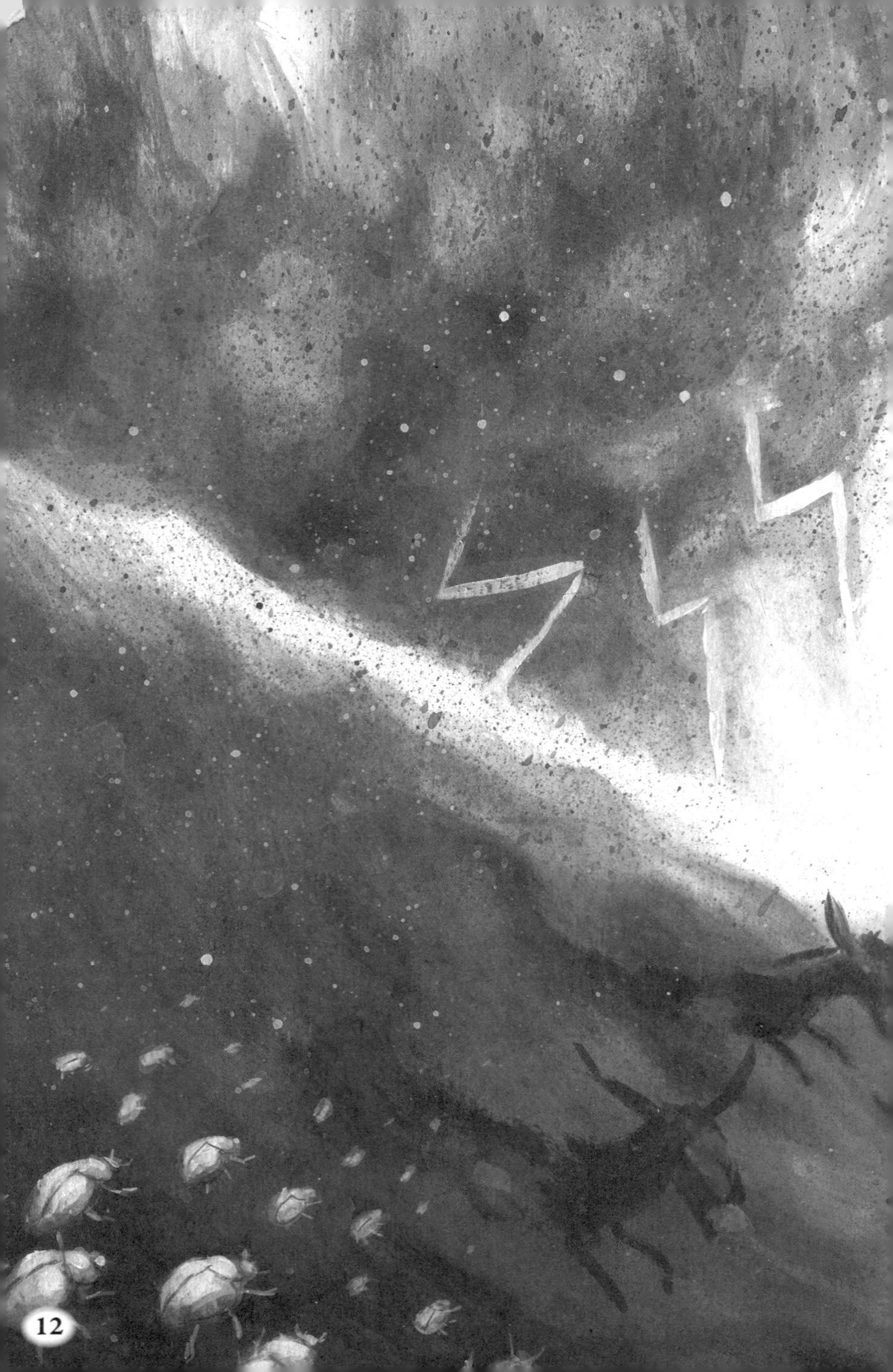

Small cracks opened up in the rocks. Out of the cracks sprang thousands of silver beetles that scurried among the feet of the frightened people. Lightning flashed across the sky. Thunder rolled in anger as if the mountain itself was coming to life.

Silvery raindrops, sparkling in the lightning, splashed upon the backs of the beetles. In a flash, the beetles swelled into strong, black-coated mules.

The mules were as dark as the storm itself, except for their gleaming silver flanks and underbellies. Their eyes were wild and dark, just like those of the mysterious stranger.

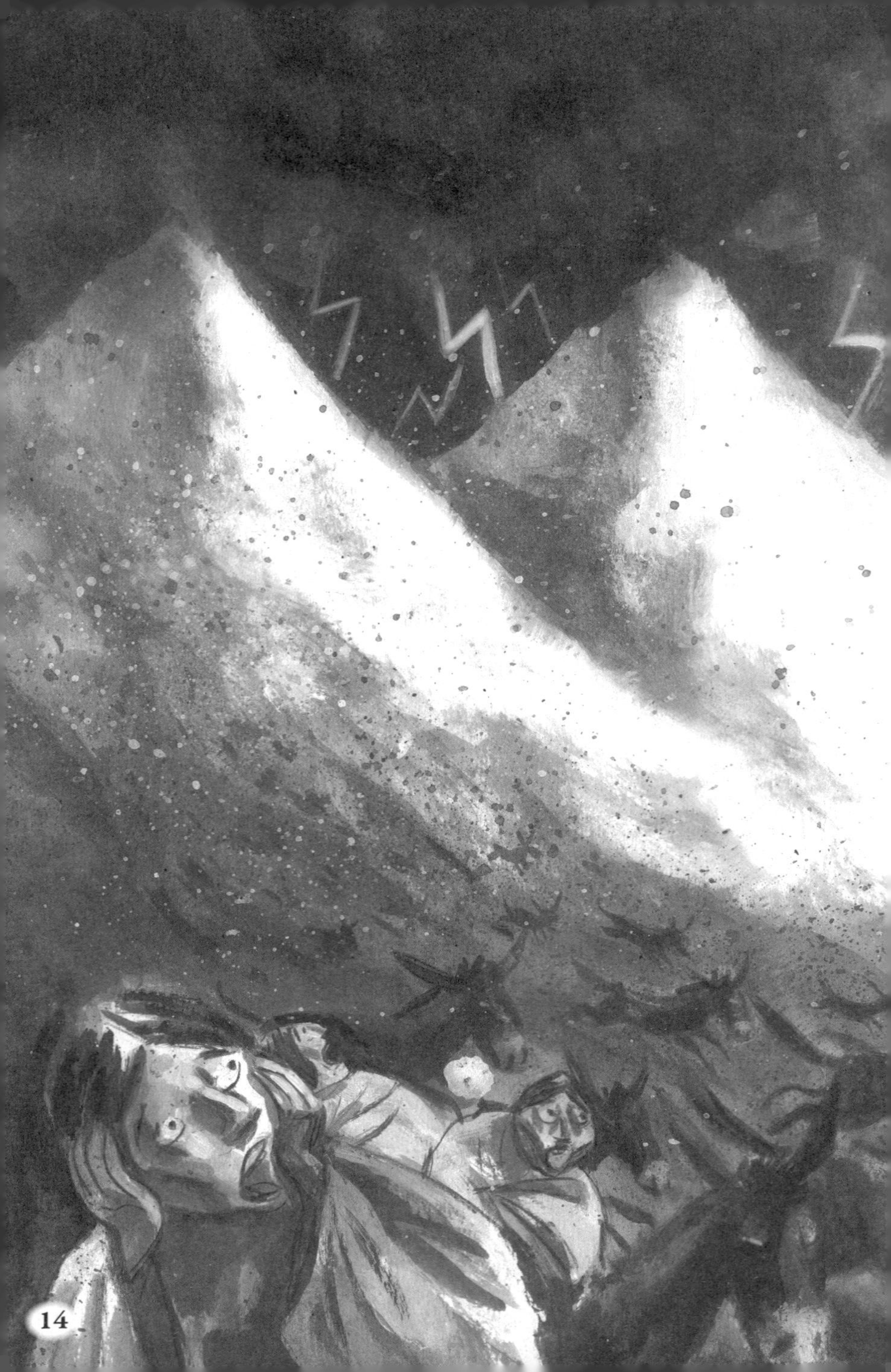

The people huddled together on the ground. They were afraid of being kicked or trampled by the wild beasts around them. They cowered in terror at the mighty power of the storm and mountain. Was Parichata angry with them for helping the invaders?

Then the stranger appeared again, riding a mule at the head of the pack. His silver-grey hair was as wild as the storm and his eyes glistened in the moonlight. With one crack of his whip the mules stampeded down the mountainside. It was like a torrent of shadows thundering downwards, with flashes of silver as they leaped over rocks and boulders.

The people watched in wonder as the mules and the stranger disappeared into the heart of the storm, never to be seen again.

Chapter 4

By dawn the next day the storm was gone, and so too were the invaders. They had found the mines empty of silver, and fearing some sort of curse, they had fled.

The people danced and sang. They were free again. The thousand years of peace had been broken, but the mountain spirits had saved them. The people of the valley looked up at the two mountains and were thankful.

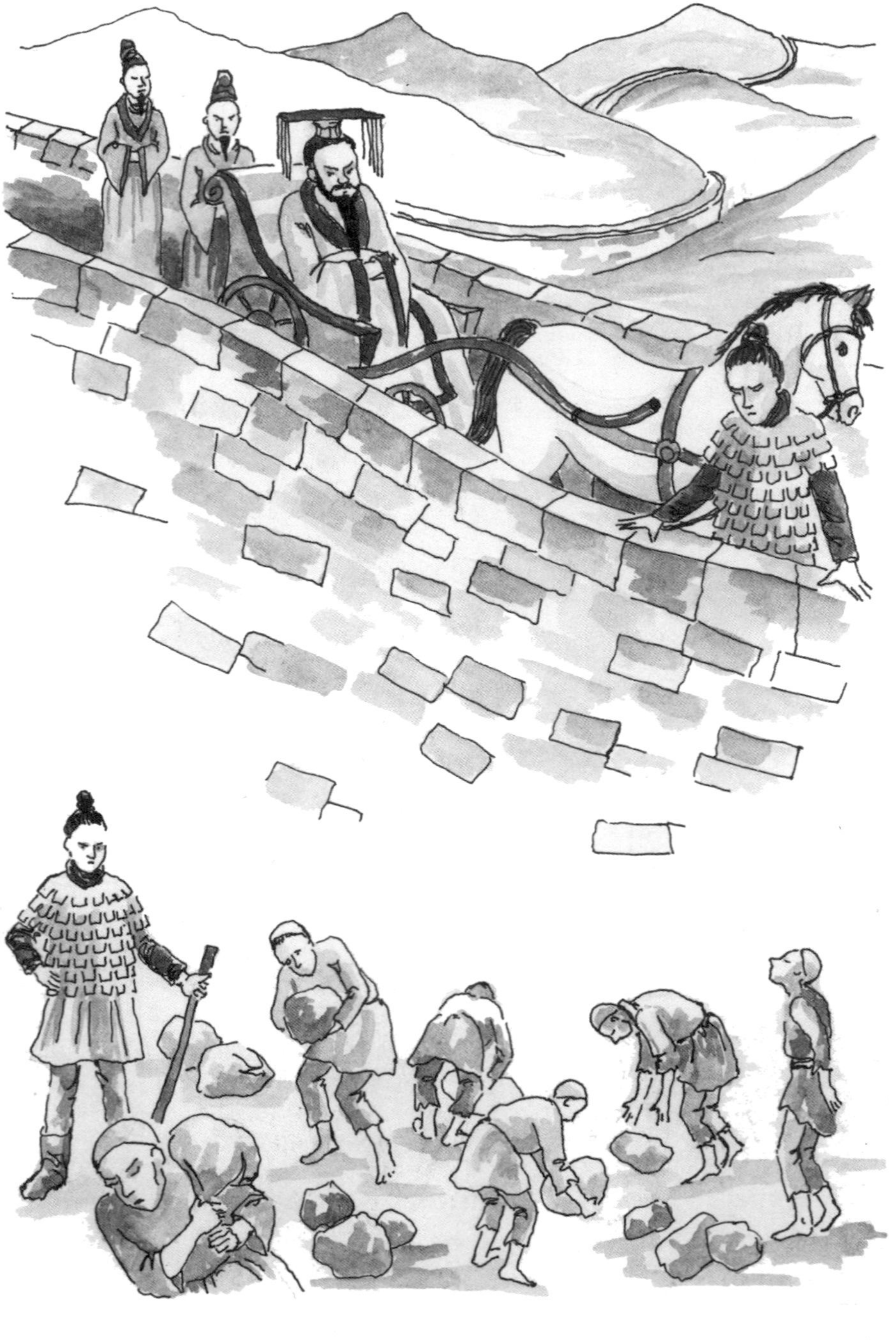

The Golden Fish

A folk tale from China

Chapter 1

Long ago, China was ruled by the Emperor Zheng. The Emperor was a powerful man. He conquered many lands until his kingdom spread far and wide. To keep his kingdom safe, he ordered the building of a great wall.

The wall was to stretch across the north of his kingdom. It would be vast. To pay for the wall, the Emperor demanded that the people should give him all the silver and gold they had. This even meant taking tiny pieces of jewellery and trinkets from the poorest peasants. But worst of all, the Emperor took away the lives of many young men. He used them as slaves to build the wall.

• *Zheng*: (say) 'jung'.

One summer's day the Emperor's men came to the mountain village of Lin Chun, a young farmer. Lin Chun had heard rumours that the soldiers were rounding up slaves. He knew it was pointless to hide. No one escaped from the Emperor's soldiers.

Just before the soldiers led him away, he kissed his young wife, Lin Han. His heart was full of sadness because he knew that he might not see her for a very long time. As he held her hands, he secretly slipped a gift to her. It was a golden fish hung on a silver chain which he had kept hidden.

'Hide it well,' he whispered to his weeping wife. 'It is charmed with three wishes. Each time you wish, you will see me. But use it wisely. Be brave and promise not to shed one tear while I am away.'

And then he was gone.

Chapter 2

When autumn came Lin Han was missing her husband terribly. But as she had promised, she did not weep. She also thought about the other men working on the Great Wall. Each falling leaf in the forest around her was like a life lost as the men suffered and died.

When she could bear it no longer, she clutched the golden fish around her neck and wished. 'Lin Chun,' she cried. 'Are you alive, or are you dying like the falling leaves around me?'

Then Lin Chun appeared before her, ragged, and as thin as the bare branches above her head. He did not speak, but she could see his suffering.

When winter came Lin Han grew more worried. But as she had promised, she did not weep, even though the months of sorrow and loneliness welled up deep within her. She also thought about the other men at the Great Wall. Each snowflake that fell around her was like a life lost.

Again, she clutched the golden fish. 'Lin Chun,' she cried. 'Are you alive, or are you like the tears I cannot shed, that are frozen like daggers within my heart?'

Then Lin Chun appeared before her. She was shocked at how thin and weak he was. She knew he would not live for much longer.

Chapter 3

In despair, Lin Han set off for the Great Wall in the frozen lands to the north. She wanted to find her husband before it was too late. She scaled many mountains. She forded many swollen rivers. She travelled many, many miles with little food or drink.

At last she came to a small hamlet nestled on a hillside. From here she could see the Great Wall. Its monstrous bulk of stone snaked away as far as the eye could see. Her spirits rose because she knew she was at the end of her journey, but they sank again at the task of finding her husband. Thousands of slaves toiled over the Great Wall, like a swarm of ants.

Lin Han took shelter from the biting winter winds in a small temple close by. She lay down exhausted. Then, clasping the golden fish to her heart once more she cried, 'Lin Chun, I am here to save you. Show yourself to me so I may find you.'

But Lin Chun appeared to her only as a spirit.

'Dear wife,' he said, 'like so many others I am now dead. My body has been cast aside by the soldiers and flung into a pit.'

Lin Han could no longer hold back her tears. Sorrow for her husband and thousands of other young men surged through her. Tears flooded down her face. As they splashed on the golden fish, the tears turned into a raging torrent that surged down the hill. The waters swirled and hurled themselves against the Great Wall, smashing it into pieces.

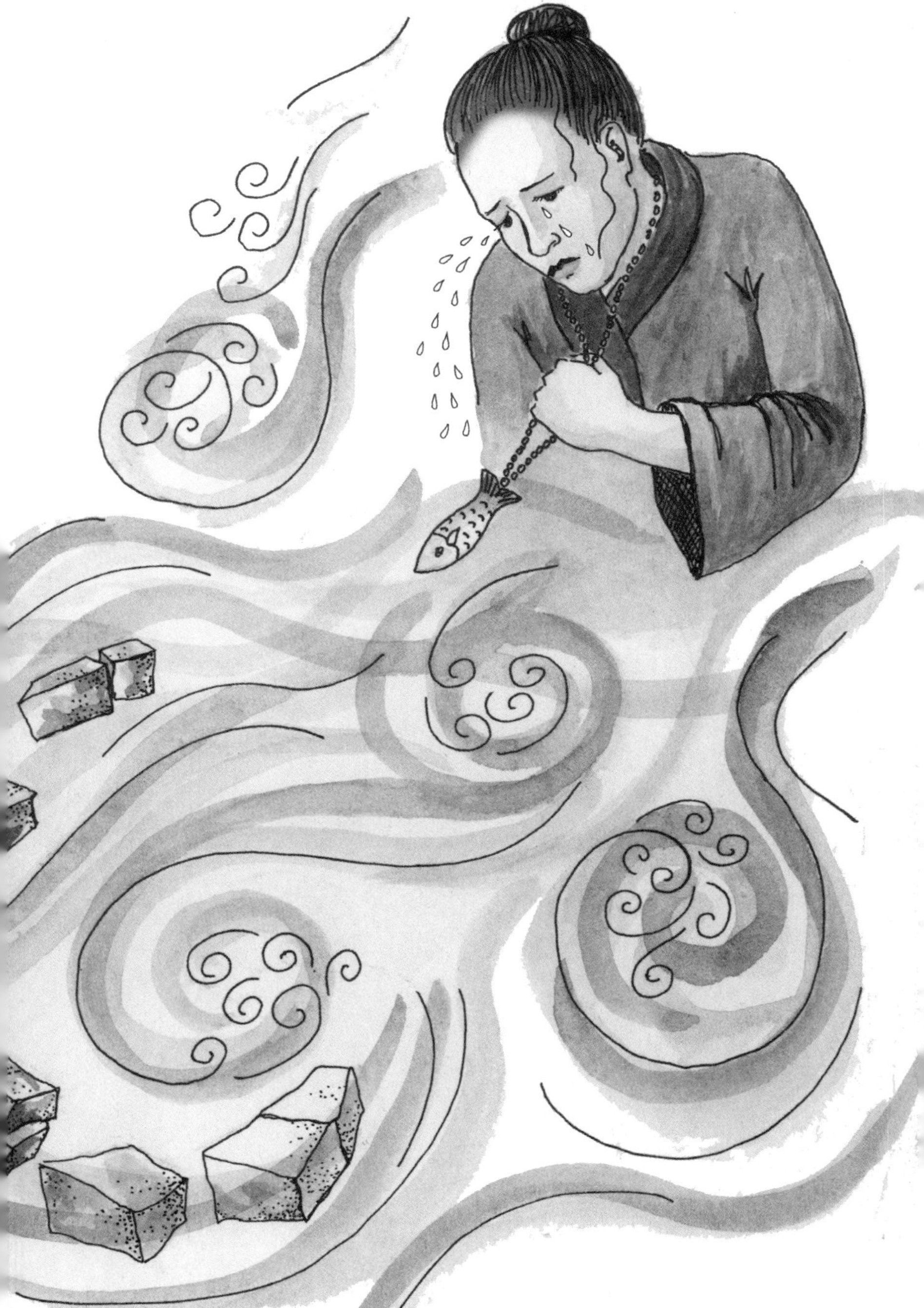

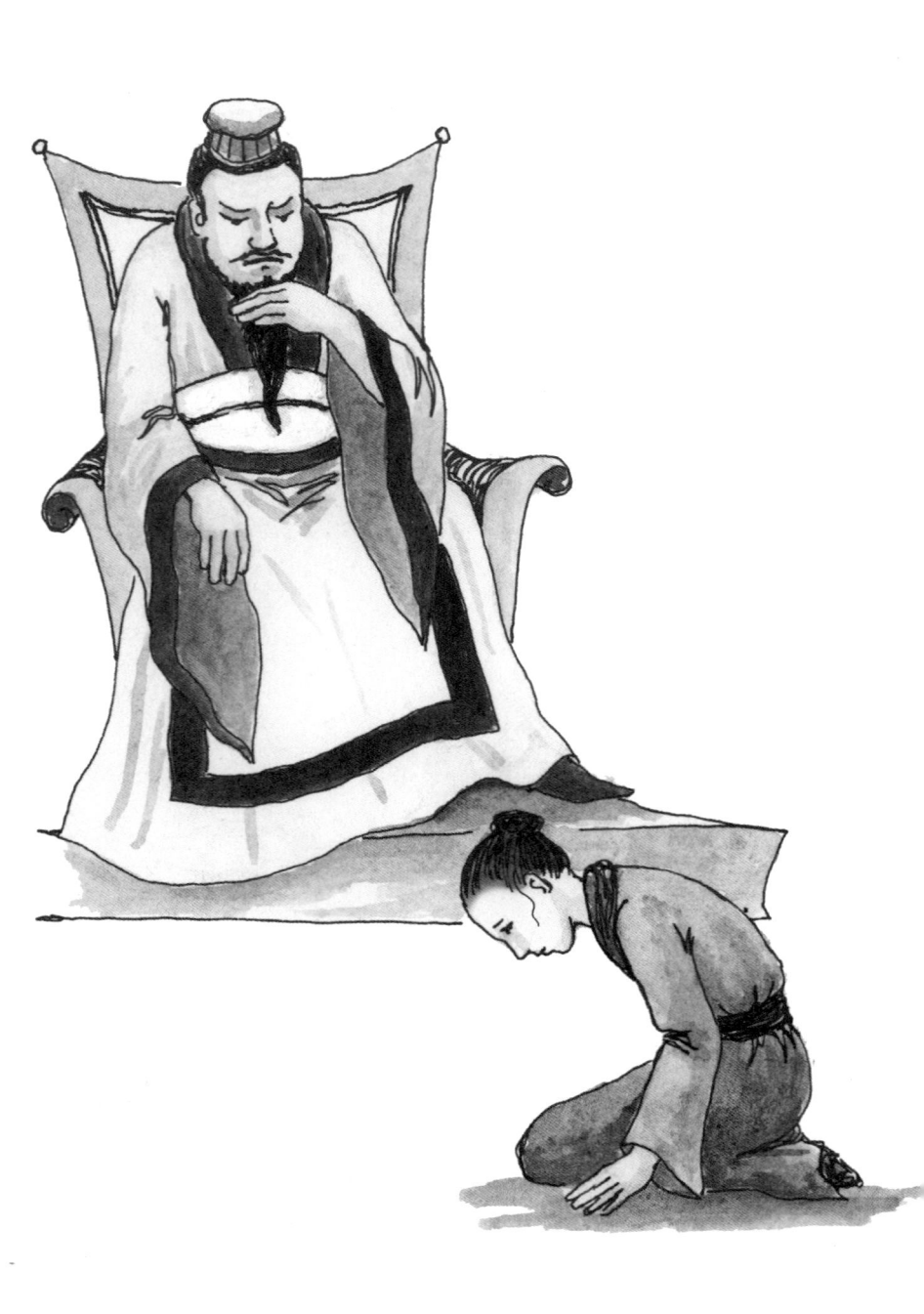

Chapter 4

The Emperor was very angry when his soldiers told him what had happened. They handed him the golden fish on the silver necklace which they had taken from Lin Han. They told him that its magic had destroyed the wall.

In his fury, the Emperor ordered for Lin Han to be punished by death. But when she was brought before him the Emperor was stunned by her beauty. He knew he could not kill her. He wanted her as his wife.

Now Lin Han knew that she could not bring her husband back, but she still loved him. She wanted to honour him. After much thought, she agreed to marry the Emperor on three conditions.

The Emperor agreed immediately for there was nothing he would not do to have such a beautiful wife.

First Lin Han made the Emperor give her back the golden fish.

Then she ordered that her husband's body be placed in a casket made from all the gold and silver that the Emperor had taken from his people. The lid was engraved with a silver fish. Finally she made the Emperor and his palace staff attend her husband's funeral. They had to grieve and lament as if he had been the Emperor's own son.

As the Emperor and his staff bowed their heads before Lin Chun's casket, Lin Han clasped the golden fish to her heart. Her tears began to flow once more, and again they turned into a torrent of water. The water swept Lin Han and the casket away from the Emperor and spilled them into a fast-flowing river nearby.

The Emperor was very angry at being tricked. He ordered his soldiers to wade into the river to grab Lin Han, but the current was fast and powerful.

The Emperor could only watch helplessly from the river bank. His eyes desperately searched the swirling waters, he could no longer see the beautiful Lin Han. But what he did see were two fish, one gold and one silver, swimming away together. They were heading towards a small farming village in the mountains.

King Midas

A fable from Ancient Greece

Chapter 1

Once there was a king called Midas who lived in Greece. He was a good king, but sometimes he was very foolish.

Most people obeyed the gods so as not to offend them, but Midas was different. He only did what they wished to gain favour and reward.

Midas secretly wished to be like the gods. He wanted to live in palaces of gold and silver and to have great feasts in his honour. He wanted all the people to worship him.

One day, while walking in his garden, Midas saw a chance to achieve his greatest wish. Resting beneath an olive tree he came upon a strange creature. It was part man and part horse. It was the satyr called Silenus, who was a good friend of the god Dionysus.

• *Silenus*: (say) 'sy-lee-nuss'.   • *Dionysus*: (say) 'dy-uh-ny-suss'.

Midas welcomed Silenus as a guest in his palace. After seven days of lavish feasts and merriment, he took Silenus back to Dionysus. He knew that the god would be pleased that his dearest companion had not come to any harm.

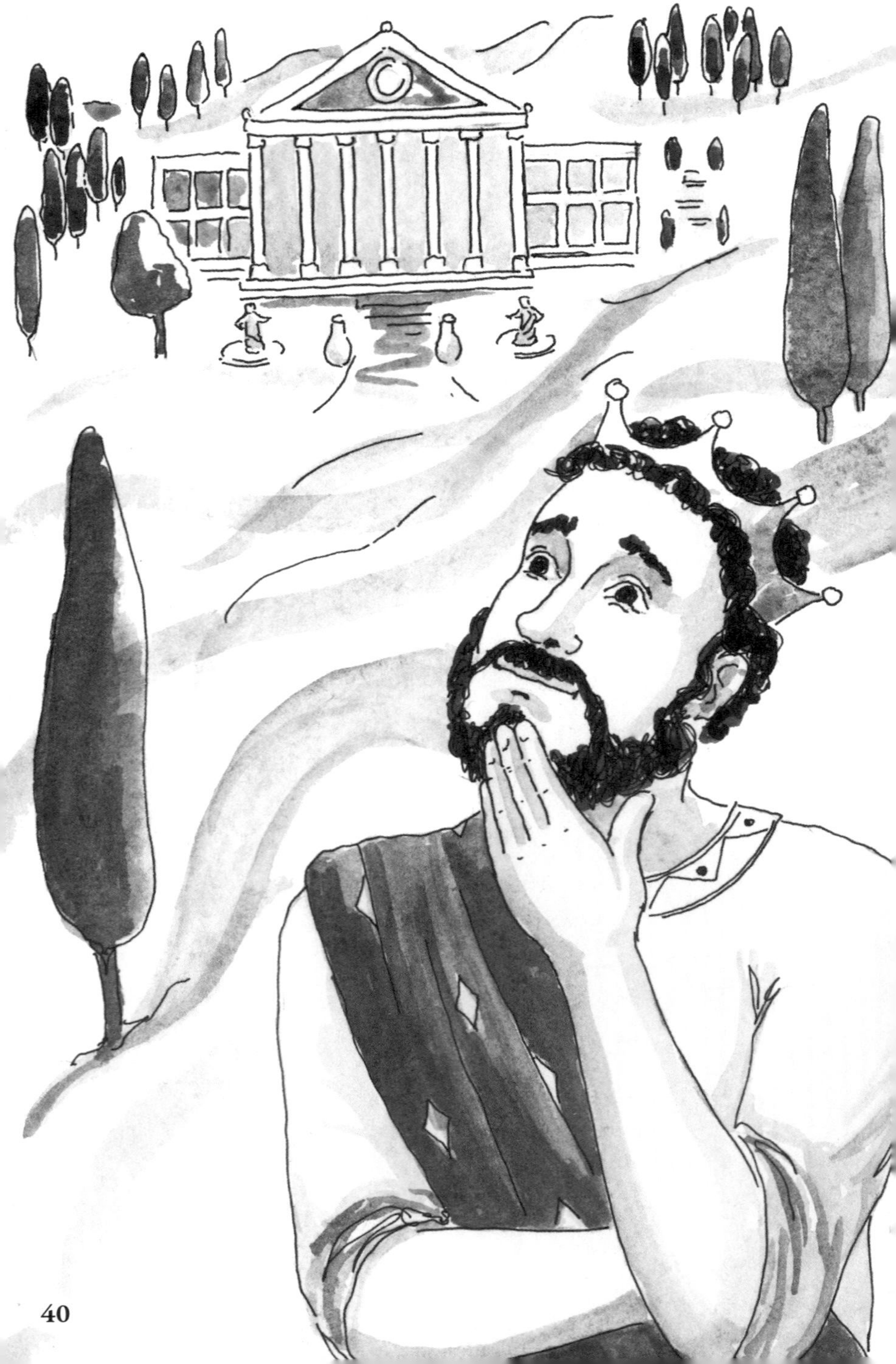

Chapter 2

Dionysus was happy to reward Midas for his good deed, but he also knew of the King's secret wish to be like the gods. He decided to set Midas a test. He offered Midas a choice: he could have a small bag of gold that would never empty, or a single wish.

Midas quickly chose the wish. He felt he had no need for a mere bag of gold, even if it never emptied. It would not impress his important friends. But the power to change his whole palace into gold would be very impressive indeed.

'Very well,' said Dionysus. 'A single wish it shall be. But think very carefully before you make your wish, because it will certainly come true.'

Sadly, Midas was too greedy and foolish to take this wise counsel. Images of glorious gleaming palaces, glittering gardens and gold laden forests danced before his eyes. He wanted them all, but to try to include them all in one wish would be too difficult. He thought he might miss something out.

Then the answer suddenly came to him.

'Everything!' he cried. 'I wish that everything that I touch shall turn into gold.'

'Everything?' asked Dionysus, astonished. 'Even your nose when you scratch it?'

'No!' cried Midas horrified.

'Everything, except your body then?' Dionysus teased. He was now having some fun with Midas.

Midas knew he had a problem. Should he make a list of everything he wanted to turn to gold but risk missing something out? Or should he insist on EVERYTHING, and list those things that ought not to be turned into gold? Yes, he thought, that was the best way to do it.

'Everything,' said Midas at last, 'except for me – and my courtiers of course – oh, and the Queen, she wouldn't forgive me for that ... and ...'

Dionysus waited patiently while Midas hastily made a list of what could NOT be turned into gold.

Can be turned to gold	Can't be turned to gold
Everything! (well, almost, excepting...)	Me!
	The courtiers, obviously.
	The queen, I suppose. Er...

Chapter 3

As Midas returned home, he passed an oak tree. He was keen to test his new power so he plucked a single leaf. It turned into gold more beautiful than if it had been the season of autumn itself.

Midas was so pleased that he patted his hunting dogs as they came yelping and barking to greet him. Suddenly the yelping and barking stopped. Instead of his loyal pets, Midas now had three gold statues.

'Hmmm,' thought Midas, 'I had forgotten about them.'

To celebrate his return, Midas threw a great feast. The people of the city flocked to the feast. They were eager to see what reward Dionysus had given their king. They stared in wonder as everything Midas touched turned into magnificent, shining gold.

47

He touched the walls – they GLISTENED. He touched the chairs his friends were sat upon – they GLEAMED. He patted the shoulders of a startled courtier – everyone held their breath – but nothing happened. Midas chuckled, 'You don't think I was that foolish do you?' Everyone sighed with relief and joined in the King's laughter.

Midas proudly told his guests that
Dionysus had given him a choice. His
friends thought him very clever to have
chosen this wish.

Happy and tired after his long journey
Midas sat down to enjoy the feast. He picked
up a chicken leg – it turned to GOLD.

Everyone cheered.

He grabbed a handful of grapes and threw them into his mouth. He nearly broke his teeth on the golden nuggets that he spat out again.

Everyone looked astonished!

A servant quickly gave him something to drink, but no sooner had it touched his lips than it too turned into a goblet of LIQUID GOLD.

But that was not the worst of it. The servant was also caught by the Midas touch and was instantly turned into a magnificent GOLDEN STATUE!

The guests started to back away from the King. A look of horror crept over Midas's face. Seeing his distress, his daughter, the Princess, ran towards him.

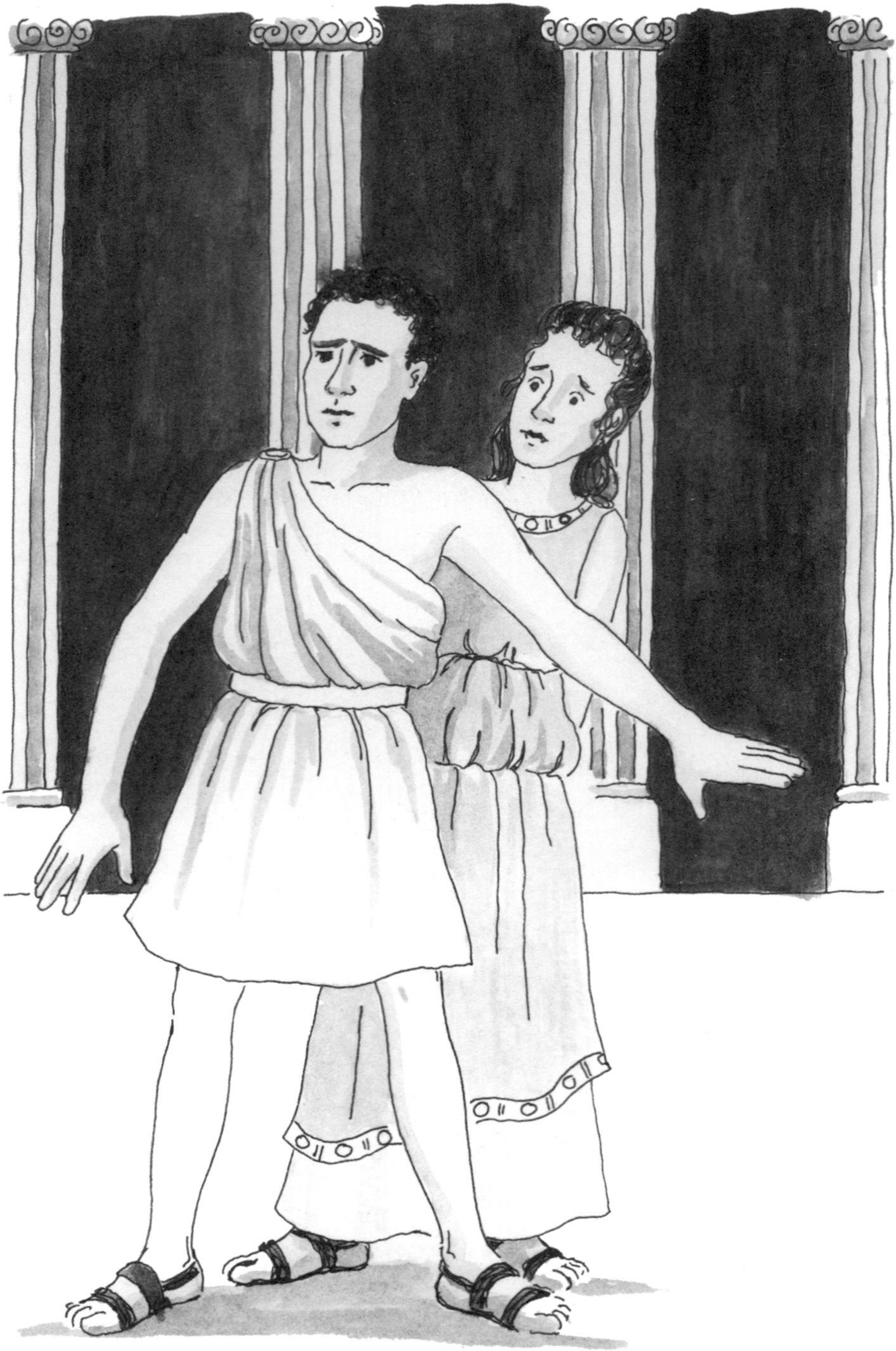

Chapter 4

'Stop! Stop!'

A young man stepped out of the crowd and in front of the Princess. He was a prince from a neighbouring land. He had arrived late at the feast, but on his way he had seen the golden leaf and the golden dogs. He had guessed that something was amiss.

'Wait,' he cried, as the Princess tried to pass him. 'The wish is a curse!'

The Prince turned to Midas. 'Sire, when you wished for EVERYTHING that you touched to be turned to gold, did you remember to leave some things out?'

'Of course,' said Midas. 'Do you think I am a fool? I am not gold. My friends are not gold. The Queen is not gold.'

'But your dogs are,' said the Prince. 'And the food you touch, and the water you drink are all turned to gold. Did you include your daughter on your list?'

In truth, Midas could not remember. He realised how greedy and foolish he had been.

The guests quickly left the palace. Everyone feared the Midas touch.

The King could not eat, he could not drink. His friends deserted him. He could not even hug his daughter. Midas became thin, frail and lonely. His wish had brought him nothing but misery.

Finally, Midas understood that being surrounded by gold was not what brought joy into his life. He went back to Dionysus and begged him to release him from his wish.

Dionysus felt that Midas had learnt his lesson and took pity on him. He told him to bathe in the waters of the river and the wish would be washed away forever. Midas took his advice, and never again wished for the riches of the gods.